Copyright

Teekwa Scarborough, MA, Newark, New Jersey

Copyright © 2020 Teekwa Scarborough. All rights reserved. No part of this publication may be reproduced, stored in, or introduced into a retrieval system, or transmitted, in any form or by any means (electronic, mechanical, photocopying, recording, or otherwise), without the prior written permission of the copyright owner.

The scanning, uploading, and distribution of this book via the Internet or any other means without the publisher's authorization are illegal and punishable by law. Please purchase only authorized electronic editions and do not participate in or encourage electronic piracy of copyrighted materials. Your support of the author's rights is appreciated.

Limits of Liability ~ Disclaimer

The author and publisher shall not be liable for your misuse of this material. This book is strictly for informational and educational purposes. The author and publisher do not guarantee that anyone following these techniques, suggestions, tips, ideas, or strategies will succeed. The author and publisher shall have no liability nor responsibility to anyone concerning any loss or damage caused, or alleged to be caused, directly or indirectly by the information contained in this book.

Cover Design – Okomota
Editing-Interior Layout – The Self-Publishing Maven and The Edit Bae
Formatting – Sandee Sevilla
ISBN – 978-1-7330781-2-2
Printed in the United States of America

Acknowledgement

A heartfelt thanks to...

My coaches: Queenette Nwobodo and Michelle Christie-Hazlehurst

Robin Devonish and Denise Sutton

Dedication

Dedication goes to my son Jayden Wright

When he knows mommy says I am working, he says, "do a good job, Mommy. I Love you!"

Table of Contents

About The Industry	6
My Backstory	7
What Is The Vision?	8
Seeing The Vision By Creating A Vision Board	9
Your Business Plan	12
Finding Your Niche/Choosing Business Services	22
Services To Offer As A VA	27
Hot Niches That Get You Paid	29
How To Figure Out Your Hourly Rate?	32
Who Is Your Ideal Client	35
Choosing A Name For Your Business	39
Marketing Your Business	40
Social Media	41
Where Do I Find My Clients	52
Onboarding Process	54
How To Book Your First Client	65

Introduction

Starting a business is an effective way to control your time, balance your life, and make more money than possible in the traditional workforce. Due to the availability of high-speed internet, people's desire to balance their lives better, and the demand for contract and remote workers today, starting a Virtual Assistant business can be the answer.

For people with the right skills (or someone willing to learn new skills), starting a service-based business as a virtual assistant is a no-brainer. Suppose you choose the right niche based on your skills, temperament, personality, and lifestyle that you want. In that case, you can essentially write your ticket by becoming a Virtual Assistant.

It is a real career where you can yield long-term profits and success.

About The Industry

The growth in the Virtual Assistant (VA) industry, since its inception in the 1990s, has been astounding. Today over 1.8 billion clients are using VA services of some sort (Tractica.com). With that type of audience and choosing the right niche, one can truly make a VA business full-time and profitable.

Of course, more people will become virtual assistants with a demand for more people to become entrepreneurs. Starting a business as a service provider has a low barrier to entry. Therefore, anyone with a skill, a computer, and a good internet connection can get started in their new business overnight.

What does this mean? There are many opportunities, but to capitalize, a niche is required to stand out. It's necessary to run a well-oiled business that easily adapts to the demand and to changing technology. Proficiency is needed to help clients modernize their processes to get more done with less.

The terms used for few names for virtual assistants are:

- Virtual Assistant (VA)
- Assistant
- Project Manager

Business Benefits of Hiring a VA!	Benefits of Being a VA!	Who Can Become a VA?
- Remote Hiring - Budget-Friendly - Contractor instead of Employee	- Extra or Full-Time Income - Work Flexibility - Home Based Business Owner	- Stay at home moms - College Students - Side Hustlers - And more…

I'll get into this more in lesson 5 of this book!

My Back Story

I remember the day when my mother bought me my first diary. It was a pink, shiny, small book with a gold-finished frame around the belt where you lock the diary with a key. At that time, it was the most precious thing to me. I wrote all my thoughts, the things that happened to me each day, and poured my emotions into whether I was sad, mad, happy, or hurt. You see, growing up, I was an extreme introvert. My family members thought there was something wrong with me.
My mother knew there was nothing wrong with me.

The ability to write down (dreams, thoughts, etc.) everything was the best thing in the world. I wanted was to become a high-end business owner. Family members and friends kept telling me to get into modeling because I was tall, dark, and pretty. Although it looked like a tremendously glamourous life, it wasn't for "me" because I was too shy. Plus, I loved my jeans, sneakers, and sweatshirts. I loved my ponytails (plain Jane, like my mother, would say).

So, let's get to the point. I wanted to become a business owner. I don't know why, but I would write how I wanted to be a powerful black businesswoman who wore nice power suits, sitting behind a big desk looking out a glass window. I often watched the movie '9 to 5'. Do you remember that movie? I didn't want to be a secretary. I avoided that path for a very long time, but: single motherhood, health insurance, and money woes superseded that decision. However, entering the working world was different from the movies I saw or books I read.
I spent 20 years working as an executive assistant. I rocked it! I used the position to my advantage and took all the courses offered to increase my skill set. I stood in my authority and always went above and beyond for my clients. It became so that managers were asking me to support their functions. I conducted Microsoft Suite classes on my lunch break to teach other assistants how to do excel, word, and PowerPoint, to name a few.
Fast forward, I move up the ranks as a Senior Executive Assistant to a Supervisor. When I received the promotion, I managed six assistants. The caveat was I had to remain in my role, support my clients, and supervise the six assistants. It was a challenge, but I welcomed it the stretch to want and be more. I went to school for IT, kept building my skill sets. I attempted to get into the IT world but was continually denied.
I kept the idea of having my own business in mind but did not know what type of business. However, having an event planning business came to mind. A virtual assistant business kept creeping up in my spirit.

It is easy to set up your virtual assistant business. You may question, once I set it up, what's next.
I could have easily written a book on getting started as an EVA business, but I am not like everyone else. Yes, I could have created an eBook to reflect my knowledge in this booming industry called Virtual Assistance. Still, I wanted to take you on a journey to become the visionary, the speaker, and the doer in your business, creating a strong foundation from the beginning to make $5000, $10,000 or more a month. However, you have to put in the work! You have to be an action taker, to move forward and get the things you want in your life.

The Virtual Assistants Guide and Journal

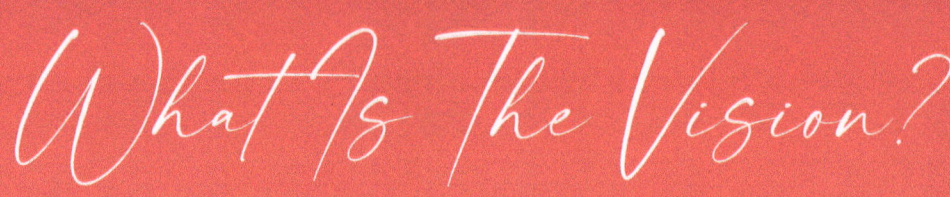

What Is The Vision?

The dictionary defines the word "vision" as the ability to think about or plan the future with imagination or wisdom. We've all had a vision of what our life would be like. We've painted a picture ever since we were children playing with our toys or imagining we were someone famous. Some of us have made those visions come true, and some of us have not.

If you've purchased this journal, that means you are a visionary who wants their business to flourish. In this exercise, go to a quiet place (get away from your significant other, kids, roommates, etc.), and work on your business vision. If you could wave a magic wand, what would your '***perfectly profitable***' business look like? I need you to go deep and provide as many details as possible.

_____
_____
_____
_____
_____
_____
_____
_____
_____
_____
_____
_____
_____
_____
_____
_____
_____

Creating A Vision Board

Now that you've written out your vision of your business, imagine what your empire will look like for generations to come. Doesn't it sound good saying *empire*? We envisioned our lives would be different from today's, and some of us have lacked guidance on what to do to make it happen.

As I stated before, I always wanted to own my own business. However, I didn't know how or when it was going to happen. One day something clicked inside and said *it is time*.
A vision board is a powerful tool that helps you narrow down your desires through what you feel and the images in your mind. When we make the vision plan and put it in front of us, it becomes more real each day. It's used for personal and business. My son and I have our travel vision board. We've already traveled to the Dominican Republic, Jamaica, and the Bahamas. Our next trip is to San Juan, Puerto Rico.

Let's get started on yours.

How Does A Vision Board Work?

Visions boards force you to explore your deepest desires and focus on those that truly matter to you. By creating one or more vision boards, we can use the space on a board, canvas, or bulletin; add pictures or words to prompt us to focus on achieving what we desire.
What will you need to create one?

1. Posterboard, corkboard, or canvas
2. Old magazines or Newspapers
3. Print out any motivational quotes, affirmations, or scripture from the Bible
4. Scissors
5. Markers, color pencils or paint
6. Glue, tape (double-sided), thumbtacks, or pins
7. Photo of yourself, family, or members of the team you are going to hire
8. Glitter (if you're like me, you like glitz and glam)
9. Sticker letters (they have all kinds of fonts and colors) (optional)

Visualization is nearly as powerful as performing the action. When you visualize yourself owning your own business, your brain trains your body for that reality.
Have you read actor Jim Carrey's story? Jim Carrey knew precisely how much he wanted to make. In 1985 he wrote himself a $10 million check for "acting services rendered," dating it ten years in the future (Thanksgiving 1995) and kept it in his wallet. Just before Thanksgiving 1995, he found out he would make $10 million for Dumb and Dumber.

Next Step...

Consistency Is Key

I have this statement on the top right of my vision board! Consistency is important. To be better, faster, and become stronger, we have to be at our best and on top of our tasks. However, by taking action every day, you will eventually see the rewards of your work. Therefore, train your body, mind, and spirit for the manifestation of your vision. The board should hang where you can see it each day. After that, the consistency in the visualization happens every time you look at it.

Let's get started.

- Find a quiet place in your home and set aside an hour to start and complete your vision boards.
- Dig deep in your thoughts. Think about the message you want to convey and how you want your vision board to look.
- Set out all your supplies — to ensure uninterrupted creativity, double-check that everything you need to create your vision board is on hand.
- Say a prayer before you begin — if you are like me, I like to pray about everything I do and ask God for guidance in everything I do. He has not failed me yet!

Consider...

- Business goals
- What your business model looks like
- Family goals (e.g., how is it going to affect them)
- Your values
- Type of people you want to hire
- Implementation
- What you want to learn or grow into

Get comfy and relax, get your favorite drink, and listen to any type of music you desire. I like scented oils and a glass of wine. Take a deep breath, close your eyes, and take a moment to reflect on your big goals and dreams. What do you want your ideal business to look like?

STEP 3

Begin cutting out images from magazines, printed images from the internet, etc. representing the type of business you want. For example, if you want an agency with multi-talented people that do websites, graphic artists, Facebook ads, and lead magnets, find photos representing that. If you want it virtual or an actual brick and mortar office, you have to make it clear and visible (get pictures of that dream building or office overlooking the city).

STEP 4

Post images of you, the dream team, and include your family (vacations you are going to take) — optional. Then, paste or pin your magazine images on your board. There's no "right way" to arrange your images. You can fill the board with pictures or just have a few posted all over on the board.

STEP 5

Use your markers or paint to write your motivational quotes or other favorite scripture onto your vision board. You can also cut out words or phrases from the magazines to paste on your board that reminds you of the business you want.

STEP 6

Display your vision board somewhere in your home where you will see it often to keep you inspired, encouraged, and ready to make your dreams come true! Kick it up a notch and put a frame around your board and hang it up. After all, it is your masterpiece!

I would love to see those vision boards when they are completed.

Join my Facebook Group **Profitable Virtual Assistants Women Christianprenuer** to share a photo of your vision board.

Your Business Plan

Now that you've written out your vision, it is time to set up your business. Most people skip this crucial part when starting your business. (Um hmm, me!) All business owners should complete a business plan. I know it's a long process, it is boring, and I just don't want to do it!

Honestly, I started my business without a plan. I had many ideas I wanted to put in place in my VA agency, but I had no clear direction of what to do and where to start. I spent a lot of money instead of making money because I didn't have a plan or a vision board (Yup!).

The first coach I invested in told me that he would not move forward with my business plans until I completed my business plan assignment. Jesus! Lord! God! Once I started, I couldn't stop creating. My coach at the time was stunned (Go me!). So, let's get to this business plan so you can set your business up for success!

You don't have to go crazy here, but you do want an idea about who your competition is, what you plan to do, who you want to do it for, and how. You can create a one-page business plan that covers all aspects of your business, or you can make it multiple pages. It's up to you.

In the USA, we have a site www.sba.gov that assists with creating a business plan. We all know that www.google.com is our friend for finding anything we need online. Please search for assistance in your country or state.

The main sections of your business plan are: Executive Summary, Business Overview, Products and Services, Market and Sales Analysis, Management Plan, Competitive Analysis, Financial Plan. There are other sections and much more detail you can add to your business plan. However, that additional information is necessary if you plan to apply for a loan for your business.

As a virtual assistant, applying for a loan is not necessary. Here is a template I give my coaching students *https://www.score.org/resource/business-plan-template-startup-business*. Why recreate the wheel. Transfer your notes from this document into the actual VA Business Plan Template once you are organized. Enjoy!

**Here is a sample one pager what you should have of your VA business
One-Pager Business Plan: Vision, Mission, Objectives, Strategies & Action plans**

VISION

WRITE IT AND MAKE IT PLAIN

Cake Made from Love Is A Bakery That
- community with home-made healthy cakes
- melts in your mouth, will not spike up your sugar, and does not have additives
- all custom designed for individual clients
- free cupcake classes for our next generation (ages 6 – 12)

Cake made from love will have many bakeries in all of the tri-state within 5 years. Serving all of the low and middle-class communities that does not have a health food store that OFFERs sweet, HEALTHY, tasty treats

MISSION

BRING TO EXISTENCE

Mission is to provide healthy, affordable and tasty desserts for the lower & middle-class communities. Additionally, use my gifted hands to teach the next generation how to make healthy treats.

OBJECTIVE

MEASURE

- Increase sales from $100,000 (2017) to $200,000 (2018)
- Open a store location per year
- Host master classes per month at $97.00 per month
- Add more designs (5) and publish 3 more cake books
- Book more sales online goal is $50,000
- Increase sales by 10% in 1 year

STRATEGIES

OVER TIME WHAT WILL MAKE YOR BUSINESS SUCCESSFUL?

- Create awareness about the healthy treats that are offered
- Sampling
- Provide information about the research and why a diabetic can get these treats and be ok, children can enjoy a healthy good treat without parents having to worry about sugar spike or cavities
- Training facilities in the neighborhood. Do demos. Attract the young children with a bright, safe and fun space for making cupcakes
- Develop a professional team that is well educated and knows the operation of the business
- Build trust and relationships by contributing to the community
- Donate goodies to homeless shelters
- Attract and build relationships with upscale clients for orders & referrals

ACTION PLAN

WHAT DO YOU NEED TO DO?

- Develop a design plan of the location
- Find real estate (every borough & tri-state areas)
- Purchase state of the art equipment
- Develop a budget for one location
- Hire staff and train them
- Order uniforms
- Order computers & cash register
- Red ribbon ceremony and open house – offer free samples

Solo Pro	LLC	S - Corp
Meaning: The owner has total control over all decisions SOLE PROPRIETORSHIP 1 OWNER	**Meaning:** Most are "member-management, a.k.a. managed by all the owners. In some (rare) cases, "Manager management" will occur where a particular manager is appointed to manage the members' business.	**Meaning:** Shareholders appoint a board of directors, which elects officers, who make the management decisions. No more than 75 shareholders must be U.S. citizens or residents, or certain types of trusts or estates.
Liability: The owner is personally liable for business debts.	**Liability:** Owners of an LLC are not personally liable for their debts and liabilities (just like a corporation's shareholders).	**Liability:** Like a regular C-corporation, all shareholders (owners/big businesses) have limited personal liability protection.
Federal Taxes: What we have here is a pass-through (income passes through the business to the owner's individual tax return). The owner reports all income and expenses on the personal tax return.	**Federal Taxes:** LLC owners report LLC income, losses, credits, and deductions on their individual tax returns. LLC owners may elect to be taxed as a partnership, corporation, S-corporation, or sole proprietorship unless they are a single-owner LLC, in which case they are treated as a sole proprietorship for tax purposes. An LLC does not pay taxes itself (instead, the income is passed through to the owner, and the owner pays taxes), although some states impose an annual franchise tax fee on LLCs.	**Federal Taxes:** The corporation qualifies for special tax treatment under the IRS (and state corporate tax statutes). It's a pass-through, like an LLC or a partnership. Any profits an S-corporation retains at the end of the year are not taxed at corporate tax rates at the business-entity level (like a regular C-corporation). Instead, they are passed through to the S-corporation's owners. S-corporation owners have an advantage over LLC members in that they don't have to pay self-employment taxes on profits not paid out as salaries.

Solo Pro	LLC	S - Corp
Can I Transfer? Business terminates upon the owner's death or withdrawal from said business. So you will likely have to change the form of the company to an LLC or corporation to transfer ownership; i.e., if you want to leave the business to Junior or sell it one day, you'll have to change the type of entity.	**Can I Transfer?** This varies according to jurisdiction. Some states holler for the dissolution of the business upon the death or withdrawal of a member.	**Can I Transfer?** Transferring corporate ownership is as easy; subject to the rules the corporation creates for its shareholders.

Do Your Thorough Research And Write Your Notes Here...

CHECKLIST FOR BUSINESS FORMATION

STEP 1

- ☐ Head on over to your state's corporate filing office (usually the secretary of state) and search for your business's proposed name to ensure that it's available.
- ☐ Go to the state's trademark database and search for your business's name to ensure it's available.
- ☐ Go to the United States Patent & Trademark Office's website (*tess2.uspto.gov*) and search the proposed name of your business to make double check

STEP 2

File For Your Organizational Documents

If for an LLC:

- ☐ Fill out a form called "Articles of Organization" on your state's corporate filing office website.
- ☐ Then just follow the instructions to complete the form (make a copy for your records) and mail it in with the required filing fee. You'll get a stamped copy of your articles from the state once they're complete.
- ☐ If your state requires it, publish the LLC formation announcement in local papers according to your state's rules (found on the secretary of state's website).
- ☐ If your state requires it, file a "Statement of Information" form within 30 days of forming your entity.
- ☐ Double-check the LLC formation requirements on your secretary of state's website to ensure that you've completed all of the necessary steps.

If for an S-Corp:

- ☐ Fill out the form called "Articles of Incorporation" on your state's corporate filing office website. Follow the instructions to complete the form and mail it in with the required filing fee (make a copy for your record!).

Note:
on the Articles of Incorporation you'll need to fill in how many shares you want the corporation to authorize (meaning the amount of shares in the company's arsenal that can be issued for things like taking on a new partner or investor). Be careful with this because in some states the corporation will be taxed based on the number of shares authorized, i.e., the more shares authorized, the more state taxes/ fees you pay. So let's keep this a simple round number, say 100? unless you know you will need to issue shares to partners or investors in the near future. Also, leave the value of the shares at "no par value" (meaning you're not yet assigning a value) unless you have reason to do otherwise. Also, know that the amount of shares authorized and the value assigned to those shares can always be changed in the future, if necessary.

The Virtual Assistants Guide and Journal

If your state requires it, file a "Statement of Information" form within 30 days of forming your entity.

- ☐ Review the corporate formation requirements on your secretary of state's website to ensure that you have completed all of the necessary steps.
- ☐ Get the Form 2553 to be filed with the IRS within 75 days of the date of incorporation. Follow the IRS Instructions for completing the form.

For a Sole Proprietorship:

- ☐ Sole proprietors are not required to register with the state. Instead, file a Fictitious Name Statement (also called a "doing business as" statement) with your local municipality's (town, city, county) business office so you can use the business name instead of your personal name to conduct business.

Obtain A Tax ID For Your Business

- ☐ Go to the IRS EIN Application Online to obtain an Employment Identification Number (EIN) for your business. Don't forget to save the confirmation letter you receive in the end!

STEP 4

Prepare Internal Organizational Documents

For an LLC:

Create your Operating Agreement. You should have one even if you are a single-member LLC. Sample Operating Agreements for each state are found on the Internet Legal Research Group's website. If you have more than one business owner, definitely have an attorney draft the Operating Agreement.

> **Hot Tip:**
> To save on attorney's fees, just have an attorney review the operating agreement that you've drafted for errors and omissions. Draft up the First Minutes to record owner approval of the LLC formation and other formation activities (also known as Action by Unanimous Written Consent).

For an S-Corp:

Create your Bylaws. You should have Bylaws even if you are the single shareholder in your corporation. If you have more than one owner in your business, definitely have an attorney draft the Bylaws for you.

- ○ Get the Form 2553 and file with the IRS within 75 days of the date of incorporation. Follow the IRS Instructions for completing the form.

Finding Your Niche
- Choosing Business Services

Discover the why behind your work ethic to discover your passion. Many VA's have not identified their niche when it's imperative to securing clients.

Steps to Identify your Niche

1. Identify **your** interests and passions.
2. Identify problems you can solve.
3. Research **your** competition.
4. Determine the profitability of **your niche**.
5. Test **your** idea with family, friends, and past co-workers you worked with.

Time for Homework:

What Passion Is Driving You To Start This Business?

_____
_____
_____
_____
_____

Complete this exercise to help you find your Niche:

1. Identify all the benefits you provided your boss (if you work in an organization), friends, family, clients, whether it was a product or service.

_____
_____
_____
_____
_____

The Virtual Assistants Guide and Journal

2. Ask yourself all the questions about your product or service you provide to your clients (if any) or if you are new - all the services you can provide to clients.
    a. How would it improve lives?
    b. How would it add value?
    c. What do you do that offers a great experience for your potential or current clients?

3. Write down all the things you love to do (this is important).

4. What products or services do you think will excite your potential or current clients? Why do you think it excites them? What type of responses or reactions did you receive?

5. What problems can you solve for your clients? (be very detailed)

6. Research the niche you identify with as your competition?

7. Find two or three VA companies and compare the prices.

8. Write down what makes you stand out from the rest of the VAs?

9. What more can you offer for the potential client to choose you over someone else?

Now align the services you provide and love to do with clients' benefits. Your niche can be any of these industries: real-estate, event planning, non-profit organizations, to name a few, but you have to know your why, passion, and meaning behind your business.

1. Specifically, who do you want to work with?

2. What type of person would you love to work with the most?

3. What can you offer this person?

4. What challenges is this person facing? What can you do to help?

Identify all the benefits/features and products/services you can provide for your clients.

A. How would 'it' improve their lives?

_____
_____
_____
_____

B. How would 'it' add value?

_____
_____
_____
_____

C. What do you do that offers a unique experience for your clients?

_____
_____
_____
_____

Write down all the benefits you provide to your clients. This exercise is important. When you are passionate about your purpose and the things you do, you're at your best.

D. Write down all of what you love to do?

_____
_____
_____
_____

E. What products or services do you believe excites your clients?

_____
_____
_____
_____

Write down what makes you '**stand out**' from the rest.

_____
_____
_____
_____

Offerings And Client Benefits

The client benefits reflect the impact your clients will receive from the services provide. At this point, you are clear on what type of services you want to offer in your Virtual Assistant business.

See the services you can offer as a virtual assistant on the next page. For now, list your offerings and benefits.

Offerings	Client Benefits

The Virtual Assistants Guide and Journal

Services To Offer
As A Virtual Assistant

Choose the one you enjoy the most, have passion for, and then list the most skills to form your services and packages.

NEWSLETTERS	MANAGE GROUPS	CREATE CONTENT	MARKETING	CREATE & MANAGE ADS
Designer Create content Automation (E-mail) Using ConvertKit Infusionsoft Constant Contact Mailchimp	Facebook LinkedIn Membership	Blog Posts Pinterest Instagram Newsletters Facebook Twitter	Digital Sales Funnel E-mail	Facebook Google Ads Instagram LinkedIn

DESIGN LANDING PAGE/CREATE	SOCIAL MEDIA STRATEGIST	WEBSITE DESIGN OR MANAGEMENT	TEACHING PLATFORMS VIA ONLINE	GIFTED DESIGNER
Instapage Leadpages Click Funnels A/B Split	LinkedIn YouTube Twitter Pinterest Instagram Facebook	SEO CSS/HTML Coding Shopify assistance WordPress Design Web design WordPress updates	Teachable Thinkific Zoom Loom Webinar Setup WebinarJam	Canva Picmonkey Photoshop Advanced Graphic Design Skills Video Editing PowerPoint Presentation eBook Design/Content Infographics Logo

The Virtual Assistants Guide and Journal

EVENT MANAGEMENT	PEOPLE MANAGEMENT	EXECUTIVE VIRTUAL ASSISTANT	BLOGGER SERVICES	MANAGE & SYSTEM SETUP
Event Planning Live Event Presentation	HR Management	Calendar/Meeting Management Meeting Minutes Data Entry Internet Research Sales calls Customer Service Order/send Gifts for clients Negative comment deletions via Facebook E-mail reminders Travel Arrangements Pay bills Various Admin task	Manage BLOGS Respond to BLOG posts Maintain editorial calendar Traffic reporting	Asana Trello Slack 17 Hats Teamwork Basecamp

WRITING TASKS	BOOKKEEPING	SOCIAL MEDIA MANAGEMENT Via online tools
Editing Resume Writing Proofreading Transcription	Payment & Invoicing Create/Manage Databases & CRM's	Hootsuite Later PlannThat Buffer Edgar

Hot Niches That Get You Paid

Currently, most hot niches surround some form of marketing, especially content marketing. Let's look at a few of these niches to get a good idea of the different types of services you can perform for your clients.

- **Social Media Manager**
  You can help your clients manage their social media. As a manager, either you can carry out the task or direct their other VAs on what to do. Also, you can hire assistants who perform directed tasks or use automation. Overall, you will manage your Client's social media marketing efforts from A to Z.

- **Social Platform Expert**
  Market your expertise on a platform such as Pinterest Expert, Instagram Expert, or others. You'll want to know the platform inside and out so you can help your clients get the most out of their marketing efforts on that platform.

- **Facebook Live Consultant**
  Today, many people use Facebook Live to market their business and expand their reach. If you have some best practices, you can help your clients get the job done by consulting on how to live stream effectively.

- **YouTube Marketing Expert**
  If you're good at building profitable and popular YouTube channels, you can provide consultant services. If incredible at editing videos, you can offer editing services.

- **Sales Funnel Strategist**
  Funnels are very popular today. Do you know how to develop and set up effective funnels? This is a wonderful way to offer services by funnel design, setup, and implementation using a specific technology like Instapages.com, to leadpages.net, or others.

- **Business Consultant**
  A business consultant works with a particular business type to help them achieve a goal. For example, you may choose to help people start a successful business like yours or help them expand in a new way.

- **WordPress Expert**
  Do you know how to navigate WordPress? If you know how to use the platform and additional software like Amember.com, or template bending, or adding new pages, or managing updates, back-ups, and security, then this is a great service to offer.

▶ **Content Writer or Copywriter**

While these are considered businesses, many virtual assistants offer services around content writing and copywriting. They may write blog posts, product descriptions, or help edit a sales page. All of these require skills in content writing and copywriting.

▶ **Content Marketing Strategist**

If you're good at seeing the big picture for your clients and know what types of content they need, how to repurpose it, and how to get the most out of content marketing, become a content marketing strategist. Manage a team to ensure all marketing goals are implemented.

▶ **Facebook Ad Manager**

Many business owners, such as coaches, product marketers, and more like to run Facebook Ads. However, creating them can be a full-time job. Creating graphics also, monitoring is required once posted. Tweaking might be necessary to fit ad guidelines. If you have proven results from ads, this is a great niche.

▶ **Launch Strategist**

Want to work with product creators? If so, a launch specialist who handles all the launches associated with a business. You would help ensure that all aspects of a launch are set up and going smoothly by using your own team or theirs.

▶ **Webinar Expert**

Many online business owners conduct webinars to bring in business and build brand awareness. Even online course creators like to use webinars to create and market their courses. If you're great with webinar technology, you can help your clients smoothly produce amazing webinars.

▶ **Live Event Expert**

If you like excitement, you can be a live event expert as a VA. You can help your clients set up their live events, ensuring success, even if you don't attend the live event. However, attending can offer a good balance between working from home and interacting with the world.

▶ **Landing Page Expert**

Today, most products have some form of specialized landing with software like Leadpages.net, Thrive Pages, or others. If you are an expert with some software, you can help your clients set up their landing pages.

▶ **Customer Service Manager**

You can be a customer service manager or provide customer service solutions for your clients. You can set up help desk software, then answer help desk questions and deal with the issues as they come.

- **Affiliate Manager**

   Another great position is that of an affiliate manager. You can help manage your Client's affiliates by getting them amped to promote products more, provide material to market the products, and troubleshoot issues with payments.

- **Technology Platform Expert**

   If you're good at setting up and using any technology in demand for your clients, you can market yourself as an expert in that technology. It doesn't matter if it's a shopping cart, a website builder, or a course builder.

Some niches pay more than others. Usually, that involves working with a niche that's experiencing a popularity surge matched with just the right services they're demanding.

How to figure out your *hourly rates?*

When you work for a company and get your paycheck, you notice all the deductions, e.g., health insurance, taxes, etc. When you are self-employed, you are responsible for paying your expenses and benefits. This is called "You are the Boss."

Income taxes, health insurance, life insurance, and retirement savings must be factored into your hourly rate since you no longer have an employer to help share in the cost of these benefits. If you aren't careful in calculating your hourly rate, you may find that you're earning less per hour as a virtual assistant than you would at a corporate job. This part is crucial to reaching the desired pay you want.

This is a great formula to take into account when setting your hourly rate.

1. Decide How Much You Want To Earn Annually
Example: I would like to make $90,000 annually after all my business expenses.

2. Now, Let's Add All The Business Expenses and Taxes
You may not know precisely how much your business expenses and taxes will be if you are a new VA. Do your very best to estimate how much they will be. Check the taxes in your state. I recommend putting at least 25% of your earnings to save for tax-time.

Here are a few things to consider:
- Accountant fees and tax prep
- Accounting software
- Continuing education courses (you need to
- continue to invest in yourself!)
- Domain and web hosting costs
- Health insurance
- Internet
- Invoicing and PayPal fees
- Laptop and equipment
- Marketing expenses
- Mobile expenses
- Self-employment taxes
- Software

According to some reports, these expenses can add to $20,000 per year!

3. Add Your Estimated Annual Expenses To Your Desired Annual Salary

Example: $90,000 + $20,000 = $110,000.

4. Figure Out How Many Billable Hours You Will Work In A Year

We tend to forget about those days during the year. In Corporate America, we do not get paid from our clients for vacations, holidays, sick time, etc. These are not billable working hours. Additionally, invoicing, accounting, marketing, discovery calls with clients are not billable to your clients. These are "You are the Boss" task.

Estimating time most people take off, three weeks' vacation, 5 - 7 holidays, eight sick days, and 25% of your time spent on nonbillable projects, you are left with about 1,300 - 1500 billable hours per year.

5. Calculate Your Rate You Should Charge Per Hour

Divide your adjusted annual earnings of $110,000 by the billable hours per year (let's use 1,500).

$110,000 ÷ 1,500 = $73.33 per hour!

Round it up to $75 per hour to make it an even number

Other ways to charge for your services

If you provide any specialized skill sets, you can charge your services by project-based, retainer packages, or price packaged

1. Project-Based is a one-time service, such as some eBook or graphic design work, event planning, or product launches. You usually charge the clients a flat fee for the projects. When you price by project-based, you must calculate how much time it will take to finish the project and charge appropriately.

    The biggest problem with this type of package is that you may underestimate the amount of time it takes to complete the work. You might want to add a little extra to help cover that, such as 10-15% more time than you think it will take.

2. Retainer Packages are a valuable way to earn a consistent income. Fees are paid in advance by the Client. This is best for long-term clients who need your help on a recurring monthly basis. Your client will pre-pay for a set number of hours per month for a retainer package, such as 10, 15, or 20 hours.

   Note: You will need to keep track of your time by only using a spreadsheet or any online software, e.g. **www.myhours.com** and **www.freshbooks.com**

   Clients will appreciate the tracking log of the activity.

3. Priced Packages are like a retainer package. The only difference is the Client pays for the package monthly. You will still need to keep track of your time and the activities. You would include in the contract that these hours do not rollover.

   I use this method for my business! My short-term contract is six months, and long-term is one year or more.

Who Is Your Ideal Client?

Being clear on who is your ideal client yields sales. If you want to consistently make at least 5K – 10K a month as a VA, completing this exercise is essential. I have coached numerous VA's and everyone I coach biggest challenge is finding clients; it can be tiresome. You should attract the right clients instead of chasing any client.

The correct way to obtain clients is by forming a connection with those who want your services. Most of my clients came via networking but began this business to spend more time with my family. However, attending networking events and traveling to different states became tiresome and costly. When my coach gave me this exercise on finding my ideal client, work became more manageable. The client kept coming because now I attract the right clients for my business.

After completing this exercise, you will connect to the ideal client you want to work with and attract. Additionally, you can craft a message to the Ideal Client ready to buy your products or services.

When you start this exercise and answer the questions, please find a quiet place to work on your avatar. Your avatar (ideal client) is someone who reflects your values, integrity and mirrors who you are (hint, hint). Your ideal client avatar keeps you focused. Have FUN with this. Don't overthink it and get emotionally drained. Keep a smile on your face and positive energy as you think about your Ideal Client's life and how you will positively impact his or her life.

These 40 Questions Will Help

1. What is your Ideal Client's name?

2. What is your Ideal Client's age?

3. What is the relationship status of your Ideal Client? (Single, married, divorced, etc.)

4. Does your Client have children?

5. If so, how many?

6. How old are their children?

7. What type of business does your Client have?

8. How much is your Client's yearly income?

9. What are your Client's hobbies?

10. What is the religious or spiritual background of your Ideal Client?

11. Where does your Ideal Client live? State? County?

12. Does your ideal Client live in the city/country/suburbs? And in what type of home? Single-family, condo, etc.? Do they rent or own?

13. Describe your Ideal Client's typical daily routine during the weekdays.

14. Describe how your Ideal Client spends their time on the weekends.

15. Does your Ideal client travel? If so, how often and where to? Do they travel for pleasure or work? Do they want to travel but can't?

16. What keeps your Client up at night?

17. If you had to describe your Client in three words, what would they be?

18. Where does your client shop for clothes?

19. What does your client splurge on?

20. What is your Client's world view?

21. What three (3) things are your ideal Client stressed about regarding his/her career/business?

22. How does your Ideal Client want to grow a year from now? What are his/her desires and goals?

23. In what areas is your Ideal Client very talented or skilled?

24. How does your Ideal Client make their buying decisions? (I.e., emotionally, permission-based with a spouse, impulse, sleep on it, etc.)

25. What fear or frustration would your Ideal Client gladly and quickly pay to have go away?

26. How does your Ideal Client feel about themselves physically?

27. How does your Ideal Client feel about themselves spiritually?

28. How does your Ideal Client feel about themselves intellectually?

29. How educated is your Ideal Client, and in what area(s)?

30. Is your Ideal Client an extrovert or an introvert?

31. Does your Ideal Client value health? What health products/services and brands does he/she like, use, and purchase?

32. Does your Ideal Client value lifestyle? What lifestyle products/services and brands does he/she like, use, and purchase?

33. Does your Ideal Client value his/her appearances? What personal appearance products/services and brands does he/she like, use, and purchase?

34. Does your Ideal Client value personal development? What personal development products/services and brands does he/she like, use, and purchase?

35. What is your Ideal Client's disposable income? (What is left over to spend?)

36. Does your Ideal Client have a good relationship with money? (fear of losing money, fear of getting rich, fear of not having enough, etc.) How is money impacting their lives?

37. Do you have any interests or hobbies that might connect you with your Ideal Client?

38. Describe your Ideal Client AFTER he/she works with you. Where do you want your Ideal Client to go, and how do you want them to grow?

39. After completing this series of questions, start shaping your Ideal Client and become clearer on who he/she is. What conclusions can you make about who your Ideal Client is?

40. Find a picture of your Ideal Client online, print it, and cut it out. Describe his/her physical appearance?

This will help you visualize and craft the necessary message needed to build your website, share content on social media, or live-streaming. You are probably thinking... More work??!!

Part 2:
Creating The Story

In the _____ (choose one: rainy, sunny, cold, humid, dry) city of _____ (choose a city), you'll find my ideal client. His/her name is _____ (choose a name) and he/she is _____ (choose and age) years old. His/her friends describe him/her as _____ (adjective) and _____ (adjective). He/she (choose one) spends the weekend enjoying _____ (list activity) _____ (list activity) _____ (list activity). He/she dresses in _____ (adjective) and _____ (adjective) clothing, and shops at _____ (list a clothing store) and _____ (list a clothing store). Overall, his/she style would be described as _____ (adjective). My Ideal client is/is not (choose one) married. My Ideal client does/does not (choose one) have kids. My Ideal client follows_____ (list an Instagram account), _____ (list an Instagram account), and _____ (list an Instagram account) on Instagram. He/she likes these accounts because they are _____ (adjective) and _____ (adjective) and they post _____ (adjective) types of photos. When my Ideal Client finds my account on Instagram, I want him/her to _____ (adjective), to see _____ (list of your products or service).

LIST OF ADJECTIVES

Adorable	Entertaining	Loveable	Silly
Adventurous	Educational	Naughty	Tender
Beautiful	Fancy	Nice	Thoughtful
Bright	Friendly	Obedient	Uptight
Calm	Gentle	Outrageous	Vivacious
Cautious	Glamorous	Poised	Valuable
Cheerful	Happy	Powerful	Wild
Defiant	Helpful	Quaint	Witty
Delightful	Important	Real	Young
Encouraging	Joyful	Selfish	Zealous
Energetic	Lazy	Shy	

The Ideal Client

 # 1 Goal: Top Problem That You Help Solve

 # 2 Goal: Second Top Problem You Help Solve

Picture Of Ideal Client

Goal #1 Challenge: What's the #1 thing getting in your Ideal Client's way?

Goal #2 Challenge: What is the #2 thing getting in your Ideal Client's way?

Finish this prompt:

I help _____
(Goal #1) _____ and (Goal #2) _____ to
avoid (Challenge #1) _____ and (Challenge #2) _____ in
_____(weeks, months).

Choosing A Name

Choosing a name for your business can be challenging because you want a different, unique name, and it stands for something. When I chose my business name, I gathered all the people who knew me, supported me, and understood my business's nature to ask them for feedback.

Things to consider when choosing a name:

- Avoid hard-to-spell names
- Do not pick a name to one specific thing you do (e.g., Gloria's transcription). Doing this will limit your company growth and remain branded in that one space
- Check other VA business names to get inspiration
- Use a name with some meaning behind it
- Get feedback
- Make sure it is a name people can pronounce and remember

Try Any Of The Options Below To Help You Get The Name For Your Business

- ▶ Poll
- ▶ Survey
- ▶ Business name party

List All The Possible Names You Can Think Of That Will Represent You And Your Business Here:

1. _____
2. _____
3. _____
4. _____
5. _____

After you settled on the name

- Search the name the (database at www.) to see if the name is available
- You also want to check to see if the domain name is available too. If so, buy the domain immediately (.com preferably). You can purchase the domain at godaddy.com, networksolutions.com or namecheap.com, or any other site you prefer
- Get your EIN after you choose a name, then apply with your city, state, and county (when applicable) for a business license
- Set up your business bank account (must have EIN), deposit your startup money, and keep all personal and business accounts separate

The Virtual Assistants Guide and Journal

Marketing

Marketing is a must for potential clients to get to know you. Develop your branding materials such as colors, fonts, and logos. Set up your website, social media accounts, e-mail, and find the right software to use for each.

https://color.adobe.com/create/color-wheel/
http://colormind.io/
https://colorhunt.co/

Free Fonts
- Fontspace.com
- Dafont.com
- Creativemarket.com

Where to get logos?
- fiverr.com
- wix.com/logo/maker/esh

Your Home Office Area Set-Up

If possible, you'll need a quiet space to work. Even if it's your kitchen table, you must have a place that you can depend on to get work done promptly during the hours you have chosen to work.

Must-haves:

- Copier/scanner/fax
- Desk and chair
- E-mail account for business
- File cabinet/file system
- High-speed internet connection
- Laptop/PC/MAC with Microsoft Office (preferred by most clients)
- A quiet and comfortable workspace
- Social networking profile
- Some clients require a landline (Headset for hands-free talk)
- A telephone number for business

Social Media

A professional social networking profile is part of branding yourself as a virtual assistant. Business owners from, e.g., corporation, entrepreneur, etc. will check your social media accounts to get an idea of who you are. So, having professional profiles helps create a positive picture.

The Best Social Media Platforms Used By Virtual Assistants Include:

- ▶ Facebook
- ▶ LinkedIn
- ▶ Pintetrest
- ▶ Twitter

Social Media Profile Set Up:

Picture (Image)

Choose a profile picture that is a professional and an up-to-date representation of you/your brand. There are a few factors to consider when choosing the right images to set up your social presence successfully:

Profile

A profile acts as a brief but insightful description of a person or an organization. Your profile is an effective way to connect with your audience and communicate clearly who you in a snapshot. A profile has several elements:

1. Name (Handle) is the name chosen to represent a person or business. The name selected for your social media profiles should align with your company and brand.

2. Represent your profile:
   - A high-resolution headshot
   - Ensure the image is taken in front of a white (or neutral) background
   - Make sure you are smiling

Bio (Description) should aim to demonstrate who you are, get an understanding of your business, interests, and the services you provide (as applicable). The biography should also contain a compelling statement, up-to-date contact information, links to your website(s), blog posts, and other social sites with clickable links (Http://).

Once complete, and you have read over what you've created, answer these questions below.

Once complete, and you have read over what you've created, answer these questions below.

- Have I chosen a strong name (handle) that reflects who I am?
- Have I included an impactful opening statement?
- Have I included my professional details?
- Have I included how my audience can contact me?
- Other social media sites?

Sample Agreement For VA Services

This agreement is made effective as of

[Date]

By and between:

Client Name
Client Address
Client E-mail

And

Executive VA Business Support Services
Your Address
Your E-mail

In this agreement, the party contracting to receive services is the "Client," and the party providing the services is the "Consultant."

The Client desires to have services provided by the Consultant. Therefore, the parties agree as follows:

Description of Services
Beginning on [date], the Consultant will provide the following services (collectively, "Services") including but not limited to:

- Various Internet research tasks
    - Finding relevant links and articles for blog
    - Competitive industry research for client projects and marketing
    - Stock photography/art research through various relevant websites
    - Compiling scheduling info for networking events
- Light Document Editing
    - Using Adobe and Office products as needed
- Project Management Assistance
- Various other services as agreed upon by both parties

The Consultant will provide Services on time as required by the Client unless otherwise agreed upon by both parties.

Payment

The Consultant will provide Services to the Client at a retainer rate of $[xx.00] per hour based on 25 hours per month. Payments for the month must be in advance to the Consultant. The Consultant will provide the Client with a weekly timesheet. Payment terms may change if agreed upon and signed by both the Client and the Consultant.

Outstanding Invoices (if applicable)

If the Client has an outstanding invoice, the charges shall accrue as follows:

30 days past due: 5 percent interest fee added to the total amount owed

45 + days past due: The Consultant will cease all services, and this agreement will be placed "on hold" until the Client has paid the total amount owed plus all applicable interest fees.

Reimbursement of Expenses

The Consultant shall be entitled to reimbursement for the following out-of-pocket expenses if the Client expressly authorizes the expenses ahead of time. (Copies of all receipts will be provided to the Client to substantiate reimbursement of expenses.)

- Postage
- Delivery/Shipping Fees
- Copying
- Printing and artwork
- Project related long distance telephone calls
- Other authorized expenses purchased solely for the Client

Support Services

At this time, no support staff is needed for the Client's projects. Should the need arise, the Client will be informed ahead of time that outsourcing or sub-contracting may be required. The Client and the Consultant will discuss options as the need arises.

Term/Termination

This agreement shall be effective until either party terminates the agreement by providing thirty (30) days written notice to the other party.

Relationship of Parties

Both parties understand that the Consultant is an Independent Contractor and is not an Employee of the Client. The Client will not provide benefits, including health insurance, paid vacation, or any other Employee benefit for the Consultant. The Consultant is also responsible for her taxes and other withholdings from her payments.

Confidentiality

The Consultant recognizes that the Client has and will have the following proprietary information:

- Products
- Prices
- Costs
- Discounts
- Future plans
- Client database
- Business affairs
- Personal information

Other information (collectively), which is valuable, special, and unique assets of the Client, the Consultant agrees not to, at any time or in any manner, either directly or indirectly, use any Information for Consultant's benefit. The consultant promises not to divulge, disclose, or communicate any information to a third party without the Client's prior written consent. The Consultant will protect the Information and treat it as strictly confidential. A violation of this article shall be a material violation of this Agreement.

Confidentiality After Termination

The confidentiality provisions shall remain in full force and effect after the termination of this Agreement.

Return Of Records

Upon termination of this Agreement, the Consultant shall deliver all records, notes, data, memoranda, models, and equipment of any nature that are in the Consultant's possession or under the Consultant's control and that are the Client's property or relate to the Client's business.

Entire Agreement

This Agreement contains the parties' entire agreement, and there are no other promises or conditions in any additional agreement, whether oral or written. This Agreement supersedes any prior written or oral agreement between the parties.

Amendment

This Agreement may be modified or amended if the amendment is in writing and signed by both parties.

Notices

All notices required or permitted under the Agreement shall be in writing and shall be deemed delivered when delivered by facsimile, in person, or deposited in the United States mail, postage prepaid, to the intended party's current mailing address.

Both parties will alert the other of a change in contact information.

Severability

If any provision of this Agreement shall be held to be invalid or unenforceable for any reason, the remaining provisions shall continue to be valid and enforceable. Suppose a court finds that any provision of the Agreement is invalid or unenforceable, but that by limiting such provisions, it would become valid and enforceable. In that case, such provision shall be deemed to be written, construed, and enforced as so limited.

Waiver Of Contractual Right

The failure of either party to enforce any provision of this Agreement shall not be construed as a waiver or limitation of that party's right to subsequently enforce and compel strict compliance with every provision of this Agreement.

Applicable Law

This Agreement shall be governed by the laws of the State of [xxx], the Consultant's state of business registration.

Client Signature _____
Date _____
Title _____
Consultant Signature _____
Date _____
Title _____

Sample Client Questionnaire And Intake

Name: _____

Email: _____

Telephone: _____   Mobile # _____

How many employees do you have? _____

What niche or industry do you serve? _____

What type of business do you have? _____

Do you use Dropbox?   ◯ Yes   ◯ No

Do you use Google Docs?   ◯ Yes   ◯ No

Who does your VA have to work with on your team?

◯ Other VAs
◯ Graphic Designer
◯ Web Designer
◯ Bookkeeper
◯ Other

_____

What social media do you use?
Please select all that apply:

◯ Facebook
◯ Twitter
◯ LinkedIn
◯ Other

_____

Any other type of online Project Management service? *(Fill in below:)*

_____

How do you want to communicate with your new VA?

- ◯ Zoom
- ◯ Google Hangouts
- ◯ Phone
- ◯ Email
- ◯ Other

_____

Will you require your VA to sign a Non-Disclosure or Confidentiality agreement? ◯ Yes   ◯ No

What services are you looking for from your VA?

- ◯ Electronic filing
- ◯ Event/Meeting planning
- ◯ E-mail Marketing
- ◯ Calendar Management
- ◯ E-mail Management
- ◯ Internet research
- ◯ Project Management and coordination
- ◯ Follow up w/leads

- ◯ Social networking management (Setting up your Facebook Fan Page, LinkedIn, Twitter, etc.)
- ◯ Template or document creation
- ◯ Editing/Proofreading
- ◯ Other
- ◯ _____
- ◯ _____

Any other type of online Project Management service? *(Fill in below:)*

_____

_____

What are you looking for in your new VA?

- Taking over specific tasks?   ◯ Yes   ◯ No
- Helping more with overall business management, brainstorming, and advice? ◯ Yes   ◯ No

How many hours are you looking to hire your new VA?

10 hours for $ _____

20 hours for $ _____

The Virtual Assistants Guide and Journal

The Launch

I am operating as a (Sole Proprietor, LLC, or SCorp)
_____

Business Name: _____

Website Domain: _____

Starting Hourly Rate: $ _____

How many hours do I want to work per week? _____

Top 3 VA Services I want to Offer
1. _____
2. _____
3. _____

Top 3 VA Services I want to Offer
[*Insert Story you created*]
_____
_____
_____
_____

My Company Mission Statement
_____
_____
_____
_____

The Virtual Assistants Guide and Journal

My Packages

Name Package #1 _____

Price Package _____
Includes what services

_____
_____
_____
_____
_____

Name Package #2 _____

Price Package _____
Includes what services

_____
_____
_____
_____
_____

Name Package #3 _____

Price Package _____
Includes what services

_____
_____
_____
_____
_____

Checklist For FREE Resources

Invoice/Payments:

☐ **PayPal**

By registering your credit card or bank account with your **PayPal** account, you can send payments using the Send and Request Money button. The money will be credited to the recipient's account and then transferred to a bank account or used to make a payment.

Note: Fees are attached to every transaction

☐ **Wave**

Wave is FREE accounting software that lets you send unlimited invoices for free to your clients. Their processing fee is standard, and you can easily accept credit card payments.

☐ **QuickBooks**

QuickBooks is a small business accounting software used to manage sales and expenses and keep track of daily transactions. You can use it for invoicing customers, paying bills, and generating reports for planning, tax filing, and more.

Note: Free trial for 30 days, and they usually have ½ prices offer at the end of the trial for the first 2 – 3 months of continuing their services

Project Management Tool

These are FREE project management tools to organize clients and projects in a visual board or format. You can add clients to the boards individually so that everyone stays on the same page

☐ Trello (Most VAs love)
☐ Asana
☐ Slack

Social Media Business Page Set up checklist

☐ Facebook
☐ Instagram
☐ LinkedIn
☐ Pinterest

Name of your handle _____ (they should all be the same across all platforms to make it easy for clients to find you)

Where Do I Find Clients?

Test Run...

If you are a new VA or trying out a new service, I find doing a test run works great! Test run some of your skills, give a sample of your services for a FREE or modest cost in return for feedback, testimonials, or add their e-mail to your e-mail list. Once you receive the feedback, you can improve on that specific skill or service. If the service was excellent, then you can ask for a testimonial. The bonus boosts your confidence level to get out there and market your services to the world.

Consider this before you start the testing:

1. What type of services you want to offer?
2. Begin building a process to take your clients through (this way, you can get the feedback on the process and tweak where needed) – Are they going to fill out a form? Discovery call? Contract?
3. Does this person fit in as your Ideal Client?
4. How long will the test run be?
5. How many testers do you plan to work with?
6. Is the tester in the industry you want to work in?
7. Find someone with a huge following to get referrals.

Where do I find the Testers?

1. Past Employers.
2. Facebook Groups.
3. Friends and Family with businesses.
4. Meet Ups.
5. Networking.

Other ways to find clients...

I believe VA's should also create a LinkedIn account. If presently have an account, make sure all information is up to date with jobs, skill, volunteerism, and experience you offer.

What else do you need?

Elevator Pitch:

A simple conversation between two people to quickly let people know what your expertise is. This is an excellent practice attending networking events. The pitch should entail the following:

1. **Who Are You, And Who Do You Serve?**

Example: I am a Virtual Assistant Branding Coach. I help Aspiring, New, and Seasoned VAs make consistent monthly income.

2. **What Is Your WHY?**

Example: My greatest passion is to provide strategies and guidance to virtual assistants that desire to attract high-paying clients who want to hire High-End Virtual Executive Assistants.

3. **What Is Unique About You?**

Example: In addition to using my strategies to attract and retain clients, I also help my clients explore options to expand on growing their businesses and becoming six-figure earners.

4. **What Is Your CTA (call to action)?**

Example: Are you ready to take your Virtual Assistant business to the next level?

Note: Schedule the call right at that moment. Use the technology you have to act quickly.

5. **Practice, Practice, And More Practice.**

Get your elevator pitch done and rehearse with family, friends, in front of the mirror, or perhaps the cat or dog. Time yourself. As your business grows and you meet more people, your elevators pitch with change over time.

Note: Do not add on anything extra to your elevator pitch that would extend the time. Make sure you stay within the 30 seconds or less range.

Recap:

I am a [List Who You Are], I Help [List Who You Serve]. One of my greatest passions is [Insert Passion Here]. I am blessed to [List the Biggest Problems You've Solved or Accomplishments]. Have You Ever [Ask a Question].

Onboarding Process

Organizational skills will go a long way when you start your VA business. The onboarding process for your clients should be an effortless, easy process for your clients. Less is best for busy business owners.

Pre-onboarding

Your potential clients will discover you via your website, referral, social media, etc. Your first move will be to have a discovery call to help them learn more about you and the services offered. Calls can be set up via Zoom, Google Hangout, or free conference call (*www.freeconferencecall.com*) or *uberconference.com*

I work a full-time job, and running my business is challenging. I desire to be a full-time entrepreneur, so I do what I must. Therefore, most of my discovery calls happen via conference call. If able to schedule a Zoom call, it is on my lunch hour. I share this to say you can run a VA business while working a part-time or full-time job.

Letting your clients hear you, or even better, see you via video, will make sure they know you're a human being who will handle their business needs with great care.

Clients can book you via free online services like Calendly or Acuity to choose dates and availability times. This eliminates going back and forth over e-mail multiple times to select a call date and time.

You can also send an e-mail before the appointment asking for the info below:

▶ Send link to a questionnaire (you can use a simple google form)

▶ Questions to ask on call:
- Business Name
- How many hours needed
- What challenges are they having?
- What duties are needed
- Other

▶ Client agrees to move forward – Move to onboard sequence

▶ The client doesn't agree to move forward – What happens? Is there a follow up in the future?

Here Is What You Do Before The Phone Call:

▶ Research your Client via their website, social media, blogs, etc.

▶ Prepare for the call
- Notes from research, what resonated with you about this Client, is this person your ideal Client, go over the pre-questions you sent
- What can you help this Client with or make an impact?

When you prepare yourself for the call and do your research, you will make a great impression.

Come to the call with probing questions and feedback.

Here are a few questions you might want to ask if the topics aren't covered during the natural conversation:

What made you start your business?
What are your current goals?
Who is your Ideal Client?
What do you want in a VA?
What is your preferred method of communication?
How often do you want to communicate with your VA?

A tip I give my coaching students is: Do not be anxious or sound desperate and lowball yourself to book a client. If they are not your Ideal Client, you do not have to take them on. The discovery call is for you and the Client to see if there is synergy and a good fit.

Note: I highly recommend not sharing prices right away. When that time comes, professionally explain your packages and the benefit. If they ask for the price upfront, kindly say that you would like to ask a few questions to get to know them and their business, and you can follow up with them with a proposal. This will help you, so you do not waste your time on a call from someone who just wants to know the cost.

Make Sure You Take Notes:

I take notes and record all my calls. I like to recap and listen to the recordings to help see where I may need conferencing improvement. A recording will also help you send an e-mail to the potential Client with all the information you promised. Taking good notes shows that you have paid close attention to the Client's needs and understand their needs to solve their problem.

Some prospective clients aren't sure if they are ready to move forward but continue to impress them by sending a follow-up e-mail shortly after the call. This practice may help get them to move forward with your services.

The fortune is in the follow-up is crucial. Numerous people have lost their jobs or business due to a lack of following up. You can also ask any other questions you may have forgotten or thought of after the call.

Moving Forward:

Suppose they are moving forward, whether, on the call or the follow-up e-mail, it's essential to have all contracts ready to send to your New Client! Include the services both parties agreed to and your contract with the terms you discussed. Always have a signed contract before you move forward to do any work with any clients.

Send The Invoice

I recommend getting your payment up-front for the first month of services. However, if you are charging hourly rates, request a deposit or partial payments, and send the invoice to be paid before any work begins.

Welcome Letter/Packet

After you've received the signed contract and payment for your first invoice, you're ready to send your welcome letter or packet and get to work!

Your welcome letter or packet should explain any final details, or reiterate them, so your Client knows how you work, what your processes are, and what to expect.

The Packet may include:

- A letter from you saying, "Welcome!"
- What you're working/office hours are and how quickly you respond to e-mails.
- Any other preferred methods of communication.
- How you handle "rush" jobs.
- How you handle referrals and if they get any kind of referral bonus.
- How you will document work processes, passwords, etc.
- How you track your time.
- How often you invoice and how you like to be paid.
- A form to collect needed information (images, logos, brand colors, passwords, etc.)
- Your contact information.

Sample Welcome Packet

Insert your company logo above. If you don't have a logo, simply type in your company name and jazz it up with a font unique to your business.

Welcome To (Business Name)!

Welcome to (Business Name)! I am thrilled about our opportunity to partner together in business. I am personally committed to providing the best possible service to you as y**our virtual assistant**. I am dedicated to **making our working relationship a success**.
I look for and welcome feedback from my clients on making (Business Name) the best virtual assistant business it can be. I put a tremendous emphasis on high-level individual client contact.
My #1 goal is to serve you with unparalleled excellence.

This Welcome Kit is a simplified way to welcome you into my client's family.
In this welcome kit, you will find:
- Explanation of How I Work
- Contract
- Client Questionnaire
- Contact Information

Please note that the contract portion of this packet and the client questionnaire will need to be filled out by you and returned to me via e-mail.

How I Work

What you can expect by working with me

All calls and e-mails will be returned within 24 hours during business days (Monday – Friday). That means I will:

- ◯ Go the extra mile to make clients happy
- ◯ Respond to e-mail and phone messages promptly
- ◯ Follow up with clients to ask for feedback
- ◯ Make recommendations and offer solutions

Hours Of Operations

My business hours are Monday – Friday 9 am – 5 pm Eastern Time. My office is closed on Saturday and Sunday. (Please adjust accordingly for your business and preferences).

Rush Jobs

I understand things pop up, and you may require immediate assistance. There is a 25% surcharge for rush jobs less than 24 hours' notice and 50% surcharge for evenings, weekends, or U.S. holidays.

Holidays

(Business Name) will take off all (Insert Country Name) national public holidays in addition to the following religious holidays: (In bullets, please list the religious holidays you intend to take off. Personalize this section according to what works for you and your business.)

Referrals

Referrals are our favorite way to gain new business. Any time you generously make one, please let us know, and we will be sure to acknowledge you with a special gift. (Feel free to elaborate here on what is a special gift. Perhaps you will offer the Client 5 free hours or a credit towards their next retainer plan purchase ONLY if a new client is signed)

Confidentiality

I adhere to a strict confidentiality code, and information will not be divulged to a third party. All documentation sent to me will be returned upon completion + payment. I take your confidentiality very seriously – all passwords are encrypted, and I use the highest internet security level. If I need to use your credit card, I will shred the info after one use. Should the business tasks be allocated to someone internally (i.e., I bring on a new team member to support me), it is acknowledged that the Client should be introduced to the new project manager and approve the change.

Sample Agreement

This agreement is made effective as of (**Date**). By and between: (**Client Name**), and (**Business Name**) (**Name of Virtual Assistant**). In this agreement, the one contracting service is a "Client," and the party providing the services is the "Consultant." Therefore, the parties agree:

Description Of Services:
Beginning on (**Date**), the Consultant will provide Business Services to the Client. Business services are defined as but not limited to (enter the work scope to be managed by the client's virtual assistant). It is understood that this work can evolve as new services are provided to the Client.

Payment:
The Consultant will provide Services to the Client at an hourly rate of (**Enter Rate**) per hour, with a 10-hour minimum a month. (**Business Name**) billing month goes from the 1st-1st. The payment must be made monthly to the Consultant via PayPal payment, bank wire, or credit card to (**Business Name**). Payment is due before work will commence. There are no refunds given for work completed and billed for.

If the Client has an outstanding invoice, the charges shall accrue as follows: 5 days past due $25/late fee applies to the balance. The Consultant will cease services, and this agreement will be placed "on hold" until the Client has paid the total amount owed plus all applicable interest fees (2% of the balance).

Relationship Of Parties:
Both parties understand that the Consultant is an Independent Contractor and is not an Employee of the Client. The Client will not provide benefits, including health insurance, paid vacation, or any other Employee benefit for the Consultant. The Consultant is also responsible for her taxes and other withholdings from her payments.

Confidentiality:
The Client recognizes the Consultant has and will have the following proprietary information: products, prices, future plans, client database, and personal information (collectively), which are valuable, select, and unique assets. The Consultant agrees not to, at any time or in any manner, either directly or indirectly, use any information for the Consultant's own benefit, divulge, disclose, or communicate any information to any third party without the prior written consent of the Client. The Consultant will protect the Information and treat it as strictly confidential.

Entire Agreement; Modification; Waiver
This Agreement constitutes the entire agreement between the parties on the subject matter contained in it and supersedes all prior and contemporaneous agreements, representations, and understandings. No supplement, modification, or amendment of this Agreement shall be binding unless executed in writing by all the parties. No waiver of any of the provisions of this Agreement shall be deemed, or shall constitute, a waiver of any other provision, whether or not similar, nor shall any waiver constitute a continuing waiver. No waiver shall be binding unless executed in writing by the party making the waiver.

Amendment:
This Agreement may be amended if the request is made in writing and is signed by both parties. All notices shall be deemed delivered when delivered in person or deposited in the mail to the intended party's current mailing address.

Severability:
If any provision of this Agreement shall be held to be invalid for any reason, the remaining provisions shall continue to be valid and enforceable. Suppose a court finds that any provision of the Agreement is invalid or unenforceable, but that by limiting such provisions, it would become valid and enforceable. In that case, such provision shall be deemed to be written, construed, and enforced as so limited.

Non-Disclosure:
You will hold in confidence, not possess or use (except to evaluate within the proposed business relationship) or disclose any Proprietary Information. Information (a) is in the public domain through no fault of yours, (b) was properly known to you before disclosure by Company. You will not reverse engineer or attempt to derive the composition or underlying information, structure, or ideas of any Proprietary Information. The foregoing does not grant you a license in or to any of the Proprietary Information.

Applicable Law"
This Agreement shall be governed by the laws of the (Enter Name of State or Country), the Consultant's state of business registration.

Termination Of The Agreement:
One-month trial period and after that 1-week notice shall be given to terminate this contract by either side.

Client Signature: _____   Date: _____

Consultant Signature: _____   Date: _____

Sample Client Questionnaire

Because it is such a critical success factor, I ask that you take the time to complete the following questionnaire thoughtfully.

1. What is the name of your company?
2. How long has the company been in business?
3. What is your working style? Describe the hours you work, your working philosophies, etc.
4. What is your company's mission statement or objective?
5. Please describe your organization in a few sentences.
6. What problem will working with a Virtual Assistant solve for you?
7. How will you determine that this project is successful?
8. Who are your three target market groups (identify the demographic)?
9. What problem do your prospects have that your organization or service solves?
10. Who are your competitors or other leaders in your industry? Please list their web addresses.
11. Why do you believe your visitors should choose you instead of the competition?
12. Who can make decisions on your business in an emergency (partner, spouse, and co-worker)?
13. What is your birthday (month and date only)?
14. What can we do to "wow" you?
15. If you have any of the following materials in place, please forward them electronically:

- ◯ Current photographs
- ◯ All relevant username and passwords I will need to manage your business (social media accounts, website login, shopping cart, e-mail passwords, etc.) (encourage the Password Manager for your clients)
- ◯ Video clips
- ◯ Electronic press kit
- ◯ Brochures
- ◯ Presentation kits
- ◯ Executive Bios
- ◯ Company fact sheet
- ◯ Current business plan
- ◯ Company event calendar
- ◯ 12-month marketing plan
- ◯ White papers
- ◯ Press clips
- ◯ Customer/client testimonials
- ◯ Website URL and any other websites you own
- ◯ Copies of video or audio clips from TV or radio interviews
- ◯ PR wire service subscription

Sample Contact

(Name of Virtual Assistant)

Office Phone: (Phone Number)

E-Mail: (e-mail)

Website: (Insert website URL)

Emergency contact: (in case you are sick or out of the office, this is the person your Client can contact for assistance. Not all VA's have an emergency back-up, however)

(Insert your Facebook biz page URL so your Client can find your profile)

(Insert your LinkedIn URL so your Client can find your profile)

www.twitter.com (Insert your Twitter handle if you have one)

plus.google.com (Insert your Google+ handle if you have one)

Free Resources

Smart business choices are necessary for opening your virtual assistant business. Free resources are okay, but it's important not to spend money on services not needed in the beginning stages. When you start growing in your business, you must invest in some advanced services to monetize your business.

Payment Methods

Here is a list of supported payment methods you can use to get paid. Yeah! I like that.
- PayPal is widely used and accepted. (Business use has fees)
- Stripe is similar to PayPal. (Fees)

Project Management Tools

Project management tools are aids to assist an individual or team effectively organize work and manage projects and tasks.
- **Planning/scheduling** - Project management tools allow you to plan and delegate work all in one place with tasks, subtasks, folders, templates, workflows, and calendars.
- **Collaboration** - E-mail is no longer the only form of communication. Use project management tools to assign tasks, add comments, organize dashboards for proofing and approvals.
- **Documentation** - Avoid missing files with file management features: editing, versioning, and storing all files.
- **Evaluation** - Track and assess productivity and growth through resource management and reporting

Sign up for the free trials and play around with them to see which one fits your needs and preference. They can be utilized on your desktop and app on your phone. Some love Asana, and some love Trello. I use Trello for my team.
- Asana
- Trello
- Slack

Consultations With Clients

You have numerous options to connect and host consultation or discovery calls with your potential Client.
- Via Phone – The traditional way (get yourself a google phone number for free)
- Zoom – A popular platform widely used by many business owners to conduct discovery or consultation, coaching sessions, training, naming a few. It is a video chat

- Google Hangouts is another form of video chat
- Facebook messenger
- Uber Conference

Set Up Appointments

Use every tool for ease to reach and make appointments with you. Our job as VAs is to solve our Client's problems, and we want to make it as easy as possible to schedule any appointments, whether it is a potential or current client.

Use online booking tools:
- Calendly
- Acuity – I use and love this one.

A great tool, you can insert your booking links on all of your social media platforms, e-mails, and website. The tool will notify you when booked. You can customize it to provide the Client with reminders a day and up to an hour before the scheduled appointment.

Password Manager

Password Manager is a great platform that stores encrypted passwords online. VA's have multiple applications to work on and should not add the pressure of remembering passwords. You can go the old school route and create a spreadsheet, but you will have to remember to update. The password manager is used not only to house your password; it automatically signs you in to your online login.
- LastPass
- 1Password

Bookkeeping

- Wave is FREE accounting software that allows you to send unlimited invoices for free to your clients. Their processing fee is standard, and you can easily accept credit card payments.
- QuickBooks is a small business accounting software program used to manage sales and expenses and keep track of daily transactions. You can use it for invoicing customers, paying bills, and generating reports for planning, tax filing, and more.

Note: Free trial for 30 days, and they usually have ½ prices offer at the end of the trial for the first 2 – 3 months of continuing their services.

Set Up Your Facebook Business Page

See the Social Media section.

Your business page should look attractive with either a professional picture of yourself or your logo.
... Add your services
... About You section
... Your experience and any other relevant information that you want your potential Client to know
... Website
... Etc.

How To Book Your *First Client?*

Starting a business brings excitement with choosing the name, registering, and purchasing new supplies. We are ready to take on the world. However, reality hits when revenue doesn't come with ease. Discouragement can set in when trying to secure new clients.

I landed my first Client through people I know, and then most of my clients came through referrals. Although I am an introvert and very quiet, I found that networking was my grove. I picked numerous clients through conferences, workshops, and mastermind groups I participated in.

Here are some ways to find a client:

▶ When you are just starting, consider working as a subcontractor for another more established VA or VA coach

▶ Join Facebook groups where your ideal clients hang out. For example, if your perfect Client is a business coach, you should be part of a couple of the FB groups where business coaches are

▶ Networking
  - Conferences, workshop, or networking events

▶ Your community: Small shops, catering halls, event planning, etc. – Educate your community on how a virtual assistant can benefit their business.

▶ Working as an intern – Join VA groups. Some groups offer intern opportunities for you to get hired with their new clients. I do this as well with my VA agency.

VA Tools

Here are some tools to research and integrate within your business.

Scheduling/Calendar Management Tools
- **Calendly**: *https://calendly.com* | Free and Paid Plans start at $8/user/month (Free 14-day is available).
- **Acuity**: *https://acuityscheduling.com* | Price: Free and Paid Plans start at $15/month (Free 7-day trial is available).
- **Google Calendar**: *https://www.google.com/calendar* | Price: Free or $5/month as part of the G Suite Basic Edition

Presentation Tools
- **PowerPoint**: (comes as part of Microsoft Office Package)
- **Keynote**: (on all Apple desktops and laptops)
- **Google Slides**: *https://www.google.com/intl/en-GB/drive/* | Price: Free

Social Media Image Design And Editing Tools
- **Canva**: *https://www.canva.com* | Price: Free or $12.95/user/month (discount with annual billing)
- **PicMonkey**: *https://www.picmonkey.com* | Price: Free photo editing and Paid Plans begin at $7.99/month (discounts with annual billing). Free 7-day trials are available.
- **Pixabay**: *https://pixabay.com/* | Free
- **Pixlr**: *https://www.pixlr.com* | Free
- **Venngage**: *https://venngage.com* | Price: Free and Paid Plans start at $19/month (discounts for quarterly and yearly pricing).

Time Tracking
- **Toggl**: *https://toggl.com* | Price: Paid Plans start at $10/user/month (discount with annual billing). Free 30-day trial.
- **MyHours**: *https://myhours.com* | Price: Free and Paid Plan is $7/month (discount with annual billing). Free 30-day trial.
- **RescueTime**: *https://www.rescuetime.com* | Price: Free and Paid Plan is $9/month (discount with annual billing). Free 14-day trial.
- **Harvest**: *https://www.getharvest.com/* Price: Free and Paid Plans start at $12/month (discount with annual billing). Free 30-day trial.

Finance

- **QuickBooks**: https://quickbooks.intuit.com | Price: Paid Plans start at $20/ month (it depends if a discount is being provided). Free 30-day trial.
- **FreshBooks**: https://www.freshbooks.com | Price: Paid Plans start at $15/month (discount with annual billing). Free 30-day trial.

Social Media Scheduling Tools

- **MeetEdgar**: https://meetedgar.com/ | Price: Paid Plan is $49/month (discount in annual billing).
- **CoSchedule**: https://coschedule.com | Price: Paid Plans start at $20/month. Free 14-day trial.
- **HootSuite**: https://hootsuite.com | Price: Free & Paid Plans start at $29/month. Free 30-day trial.
- **Buffer**: https://buffer.com | Price: Paid Plans start at $15/month (discounts for annual billing). Free 14-day trial.

Live Streaming

- **Periscope**: http://periscope.tv | Price: Free
- **Instagram Stories**: https://www.instagram.com | Price: Free for IG users
- **IGTV**: https://business.instagram.com/a/igtv | Free for IG users
- **Facebook Live**: https://live.fb.com | Price: Free for FB users
- **YouTube Live**: https://www.youtube.com/my_live_events | Free for Google account users

Automation Tools

- **IFTTT**: https://ifttt.com | Price: Free
- **Boomerang**: https://www.boomeranggmail.com | Price: Free and Paid Plans start at $4.99/month. Free 30-day trial.
- **Zapier**: https://zapier.com | Price: Free and Paid Plans start at $25/month (discounts with annual billing). Free 14-day trial.

E-mail List Management:

- **AWeber**: https://www.aweber.com | Price: Paid Plans start at $19/month. Free 30-day trial.
- **Constant Contact**: https://www.constantcontact.com | Price: Paid Plans start at $20/month. Free 60-day trial.
- **Mailchimp**: http://www.mailchimp.com | Price: Free and Paid Plans start at $9.99/month.
- **ConvertKit**: https://convertkit.com | Price: Paid Plans start at $29/month. Free 14-day trial.
- **ActiveCampaign**: https://www.activecampaign.com | Price: Paid Plans start at $14/month (discounts with annual billing). Free 14-day trial.

Marketing Platform (CRM, E-mail, Shopping Carts, Affiliate Programs, etc.)

- **Ontraport**: https://ontraport.com | Price: Paid Plans start at $79/month. Free 14-day trial.
- **ClickFunnels**: https://www.clickfunnels.com | Price: Paid Plan is $297/month] [Free 14-day trial.
- **1ShoppingCart**: https://www.1shoppingcart.com | Price: Paid Plans start at $59/month. Free 30-day trial.
- **Infusionsoft**: https://www.infusionsoft.com | Price: Paid Plans start at $79/month. Free 14-day trial.

Ecommerce Tools:

- **PayPal**: https://www.paypal.com | Price: Transaction fee rates (2.9% + $0.30 per sale)
- **Stripe**: https://www.stripe.com | Price: Transaction fee rates (flat-rate 2.9% + $0.30 per successful transaction if you are under $1 million in volume per year)

Video Editing

- **Camtasia**: https://www.techsmith.com/camtasia | Price: Starts with a one-time payment of $249 for a single user license (compatible with Mac and Windows). A fee of $99.50 for upgrades (volume discounts for business, education, government, and non-profit). Free 30-day trial.
- **Ecamm Call Recorder for Skype**: https://www.ecamm.com/mac/callrecorder | Price: Free and One-time payment of $39.95 for free lifetime updates plus fast and free support.

Video Hosting Tools

- **Vimeo**: https://vimeo.com | Price: Free and Paid Plans start at $12/month (discount for annual billing)
- **YouTube**: https://www.youtube.com | Price: Free

Webinar Tools

- **GoToWebinar**: https://www.gotomeeting.com | Price: Paid Plans start at $59/month for 100 participants (discounts for annual billing). Free 7-day trial.
- **Zoom**: https://www.zoom.us | Price: Free (up to 100 participants) & Paid Plans start at $14.99/month/host

Creating Course

- **Thinkific**: https://www.thinkific.com | Price: Free and Paid Plans begin at $49/month (discounts with annual billing)
- **Teachable**: https://teachable.com | Price: Free and Paid Plans starting at $39/month (discounts for annual billing).

Screenshot Apps

- **Snagit**: https://www.techsmith.com/screen-capture.html | Price: Paid Plans begin at $49.95/month for a single user, and discounts are applied depending on the volume of users. Free 15-day trial.
- **SweetProcess**: https://www.sweetprocess.com | Price: Paid Plan starts at a base rate of $99/month (which includes up to 20 users) + $5/month for additional members (discount for annual billing). Free 14-day trial.

Organization - Project Management

team collaboration tools.

- **Trello**: https://trello.com | Price: Free
- **Asana**: https://asana.com | Price: Free and Paid Plan at $9.99/user/month

Created by two of Facebook's co-founders, Asana is one of the most accessible project management tools to use because it's intuitive and user-friendly.

Task Management

- **Toodledo**: https://www.toodledo.com | Price: Free
- **Sortd**: https://www.sortd.com | Price: Free and Paid Plans start at $6/month/user. Free 14-day trial.
- **Remember the Milk**: https://rememberthemilk.com | Price: Free and Paid Plan is $39.99/yr
- **Doit.im**: https://doit.im | Price: Free and Paid Plans start at $2/month (discount for annual billing).

Sharing Passwords

- **LastPass**: https://www.lastpass.com | Price: Free and Paid Plan at $2/month. Free 30-day trial.

Writing Tools

- **Hemingway Editor**: https://www.hemingwayapp.com | Price: Free & Paid Plans start at $19.99.
- **Grammarly**: https://www.grammarly.com | Price: Fee and Paid Plans begin at $29.95/month (discounts for quarterly and annual billing)

Landing Pages Tools

- **Instapage**: *https://instapage.com* | Price: Paid Plans start at $129/month (discount with annual billing). Free 14-day trial.
- **Leadpages**: *https://www.leadpages.net* | Price: Paid Plans start at $37/month (discounts with annual billing). Free 14-day trial.
- **ClickFunnels**: *https://www.clickfunnels.com* | Price: Paid Plans start at $97/month. Free 14-day trial.

This tool gives you the ability to design landing pages that easily feed your sales funnel.

Onboarding Tools

- **Dubsado**: *https://www.dubsado.com* | Price: Free for 0 - 3 clients/leads and Paid Plans start at $35/month (discount for annual billing).
- **17hats**: *https://www.17hats.com* | Price: Paid Plan is $45/month (discounts for annual and two-year billing).
- **And Co**: *https://www.and.co* | Price: Free (1 active client) and Paid Plan at $18/month.
- **HelloSign**: *https://www.hellosign.com* | Price: Free (3 documents/month) & Paid plan start at $15/month. Free 30-day trial.

For a deeper dive into becoming a profitable virtual assistant, invest in my Virtual Assistant Business Workshop *https://www.vabw.teekwa.com/* Or schedule a consultation with me today *https://bit.ly/37hxyUC*

Teekwa Scarborough, A Virtual Assistant Coach
CEO of PowerPro Assistants

Follow me on:

https://www.facebook.com/coachteekwa

https://www.instagram.com/coachteekwa

https://twitter.com/coachteekwa

Apple Podcasts Vision, Impact & Purpose

www.ingramcontent.com/pod-product-compliance
Lightning Source LLC
Chambersburg PA
CBHW061113070526
44583CB00027B/3278